A Writer's Retreat

Starting from Scratch to Success!

Micheline Côté

First Edition, 2011
Published in Québec, Canada

ISBN: 1-4563-4236-3
ISBN-13: 9781456342364

CONTENTS

Acknowledgments

I would like to thank all of the people who have contributed to the inspiration and creation of this book. I am grateful to my own guests, who have taught me the art of hosting a writer's retreat and my business associates who put their trust in me in order to realize their dreams of running their own successful writer's retreats.

Many thanks to Cindy Barrilleaux, my editor, for her trouble-shooting skills, in particular, her capacity to grasp the writing sense of a foreign-language writer. I would not have been able to get my work done without her invaluable suggestions and support.

I would also like to thank Nicole Coley, my long-time friend, who motivated me to make a commitment to myself a year ago to write and finish this book. Thank you to all my family and dear friends for bringing your wonderful selves into my life.

Preface

In 1996, I was working as a cultural attaché for the Québec Ministry of International Relations based in Los Angeles, California. I was feeling both professionally and personally fulfilled, despite the accumulated stress of living in a very large city.

Suddenly, within a month, the Québec government closed 23 of their offices around the world, and I found myself unemployed. This decision became key to my moving out of Los Angeles and to building my own art business. I had always wanted to pursue a career working with artists and writers, even with my many accomplishments in my career in communications and cultural affairs.

After a six-month break, traveling the Western states in my motor home, I found my niche and relocated in the small town of Cascade, Colorado. There I co-founded The Writers' Retreat. At that time, we were the pioneers in the field. There were several not-for-profit artists' residencies that required an application process in North America—we could count them on ten fingers—but just a few for-profit retreats with a policy of "first reserved, first served" existed. And none offered on-site literary services—only lodging. We created a unique, sharply honed niche by offering year-round short-term residency with on-site literary services to residents on a first-come, first-served basis.

Our residential retreat was dedicated to writers who had neither the flexibility nor inclination to compete for a place to write. We encouraged extended stays, but offered any length of stay in our 15 studios set in a compound of five houses nestled at the foot of Pikes Peak. We catered to motivated, independent writers. Recognizing the deadline-driven reality of the working writer, we wanted to accommodate their schedule, not ours. Was their writing worthy of pursuit at the Retreat? Only the writer's opinion was relevant to that question. We did not presume to judge the merit of their work or their reasons for coming to the Retreat. We embraced writers of all genres, from early career to those that were well established.

Two years later we added two satellite retreats to accommodate writers where our program director and mentor was conducting workshops, private mentoring sessions, and critique and editing for residents. The satellite-retreats formula worked well and allowed us to serve a larger community of writers. However, it became overwhelming for one person to ensure both personalized and quality literary services to all residents. After four years in Colorado, I returned to my roots, in Québec (Canada), where I established the new headquarters of The Writers' Retreat.

While running the Retreat part time, I got my license and

started to practice real estate. I then re-ignited my passion for the retreat business and restructured the eight-year-old concept to better meet the needs of writers. I put my "new hat" on and began to convert my ideas/vision to reality: to develop a network of independently owned and operated retreats and to focus on helping people to realize their dream and pursue their passion.

Introduction

Perhaps you've attended a writer's retreat and experienced, if only for a brief time, what it means to leave the mundane details of your busy life behind to focus on your writing. Perhaps you have always written at home or in your profession. Or you possess the gift of hospitality and a love of the arts, but don't know how make the transition to entrepreneur.

If you have ever thought of owning and operating a writers' retreat but didn't know where to start, this book will provide you with a more refined sense of purpose and the motivation needed to take action in order to make your dream come true.

A clearly defined goal and a plan of action are critical to your success (sprinkled with passion, of course!) With the help of this book, you will begin to formulate a plan, become aware of the steps needed to move forward, and map out your unique road to success. Chances are, this book will not only answer the questions that motivated you to read it, but will also answer questions you have not even thought of yet.

To help you get started, I want you to think about the five most positive experiences in your life where you ventured outside your comfort zone. Take the time to write down what it was you wanted so badly that you were willing to feel some initial discomfort in order to get it. Next to each positive experience, then write down what you had to overcome in order to get what you wanted as well as what you believed would be so rewarding about the outcome that you were willing to take a chance.

You have just demonstrated that you already know the three essential elements needed for success:

1. To determine clearly what you want.
2. To put self-doubt aside and believe your goal is possible.
3. To jump without a parachute and take action.

Chapter 1
Why This Model Works

The model I propose and the tools I offer work because they provide consistent value to clients. I define value as what people perceive it to be, and nothing more. I share ways for you to go beyond your customers' wildest expectations. This is important, because it is through the understanding of value, as it impacts everyone your business comes into contact with, that every retreat business lives.

- Value can be a word said at the door of the retreat when a writer leaves
- Value can be an unexpected gift arriving in the mail from the retreat operator
- Value can be giving an extra hour of your time for that scheduled coaching session or your dedication in explaining your literary services

Value is essential to your retreat business and to the satisfaction you get from it as it grows.

This model also works and produces results because we learned how to improve our model and tools to make things work effectively for our customers and our business. For retreat operators to do extraordinary things, a "way of doing things" is absolutely essential. These are the tools you use to get the job done in order to differentiate your business from others. It is your job to improve these tools and to produce great results over and over again.

The model works because it provides you with the structure you need to "get the job done" in the most efficient and effective way. A life lacking comprehensive structure is an aimless wreck. Structure provides the relatively fixed points of reference we need. Once your retreat business looks orderly, it will say to your resident-writers that they can trust their projects with you.

So, our tools designate the purpose of the work, lay out the steps needed to be taken while operating your retreat, and summarize the standards associated with the process.

This model will allow you to bring consistency to the experience of the retreat. The expectations you create on a writer's first stay should not be violated at subsequent visits. Do not take away what you give the customer--provide consistency of experience. Your retreat will not only look orderly, it will operate in a predictable, uniform way.

Chapter 2

Where Are You Now?

Most of the people with whom I consult on how to establish a retreat know what they want to do but are lost in the process or do not even know where to start. Some already own a beautiful place for a retreat and want to make a profitable venture out of it. Others own the property, but their interest lies in helping the writing community and sharing their place as a writing venue. I get quite a few inquiries from career-oriented people starting out on a new path.

Others are retiring professors or business consultants who want to share their knowledge and expertise with writers while creating a new lifestyle for themselves and generating some income. Some people contact me because they have a strong background in writing but do not have a building for the retreat. For them, partnering with someone who has a retreat space is a great way to reach their goal.

The situation is different for everyone, and there is room for everyone who wants to be part of a writing retreat; it is a matter of matching goals and objectives. I hope you will find what applies to you in this book.

No matter what your particular situation, I will share with you the details of my success so you do not find yourself re-inventing the wheel. As current retreat operators know, I have loved sharing what I have learned. I have always enjoyed working with creative and business people and promoting services or products dear to my heart. However, I am selective about the people I invite to join my network. If sharing is not part of your vocabulary, you might as well forget about it.

Chapter 3
The Foundation: Developing a Vision

If you want to create a successful and profitable venture, you first need to build a solid foundation for your dream of a residential retreat. My experience can help you determine what you want in your retreat business so you can experience success as *you* define it.

Believe it or not, your retreat business is *not* the first order of business on the agenda. You are. Before you determine what role your retreat business will play in your life, ask yourself: What do I value most? What kind of life do I want at this stage of my life? What do I want it to look like, to feel like? Am I seeking a lifestyle, with the income secondary, or am I seeking a viable retreat business with the lifestyle secondary? Knowing your standards or primary aim or vision—call it whatever you want—will answer all these questions.

With a vision, you can create your life intentionally, actively making it into the life you wish it to be. Simple? Yes. Easy? No. But it is absolutely essential that your retreat business have meaning beyond energy, time, or work. This is why your vision is so important to the success of your retreat business. With no clear picture of how you wish your life to be, how on earth can you begin to live it? Great people have a vision of their ideal lives that they practice creating each and every day. They live out the vision of their future in the present and create their lives actively. Most people are created *by* their lives and passively wait to see where life takes them next. The difference between the two is the difference between living fully and just existing. Living intentionally and living by accident.

I am speaking from experience. When I was diagnosed with cancer—an Ewing sarcoma—at the age of 20, I decided to change my life. What I wanted suddenly became very clear: I wanted to live. I wanted to be healthy. I have never been sick since, except for a few colds. And I wanted to travel the world. So one sunny morning, despite having no money to travel, I decided to realize a long-time dream and fly to French Polynesia to live with the natives. One year later, after having worked three jobs at the same time, I took a one-year leave of absence from my work at Laval University and flew to Tahiti. I spent six months there, tasting every precious moment with the locals, journaling, and sailing the South Seas. For the next 10 years, I felt like I had lived 30 years, because everything I did was a product of my choice.

You do not need to have cancer to ask yourself what you really want in life. How about pausing now to reflect on these questions?

> What do I wish my life to look like?
> How do I wish my life to be on a day-to-day basis?
> What would I like to be able to say I truly know about my life?
> How would I like to be with other people in my life—my family, my friends, my business associates, my customers, and my community?
> What would I like to be doing one year from now? Ten years from now? When my life comes to a close?
> What, specifically, would I like to learn during those periods of my life, spiritually, physically, financially, technically, intellectually?
> How much money will I need to do the things I wish to do?

These are just a few questions you might ask yourself in the creation of your vision or primary aim. Your answers become *your* standards. Once you know them, you can then turn your attention to the retreat business that is going to help you get there. Your primary aim and vision are necessary to bring your retreat business to life and your life to your retreat business. This brings you purpose, energy, and the grist for your day-to-day mill.

Keep in mind that there is a fundamental difference between a vision and a business plan. A statement such as

"My goal is to be the largest ecological retreat," is not a vision but rather something you might say to please your bank officer. A vision consists of the full development of an image of your target goal. You have to have a clear and complete image of what you want. Really knowing what we want is one of the most difficult things for most human beings to develop.

I can hear you saying, "Okay, I've got it, but how do I put it together now, in reality?" That is what this book is all about.

Chapter 4
Understand Your Value and Strengths

Like most people who first contact me to obtain information on how to start and operate a retreat, you may think only in terms of lodging as a way to generate income. In fact, you have much more to offer. I will help you define the value you offer—your strengths and talents. Through this you will be open to new ideas so you can better serve your residents while generating additional income. You will also understand why a writing mentor is a key to the success of your retreat.

Some writers wanting to stay at your retreat may choose to work on their own to advance or complete a project. However, a large percentage of your residents will want some kind of guidance and coaching or to interact with other writers or a mentor so they are stimulated in their project. It's important, therefore, for you to identify the role you will play in your relationship with the residents.

You can do your own evaluation of your strengths. Think about and describe your background, your career, your experience, your knowledge and expertise, and your interests. Be specific, identifying all that you bring to your retreat business. You may already provide literary critique, literary coaching/mentoring, and editing in your daily work. You may conduct workshops in fiction, nonfiction, screenwriting, or playwriting. Perhaps you have been writing a journal for several years and would like to share your experience with others and guide them to do same.

Some residents may want assistance defining their writing project, establishing a plan, figuring out where to start, or writing a synopsis. Others may want feedback on their writing on a daily basis. Others may need guidance writing query letters or book proposals, advice on publishing and self-publishing and promoting their work. That is where an on-site mentor plays an important role in this business. You do not have to have a degree in literature to assist your residents. Just remember the strengths you have identified through your evaluation. Being a good listener is certainly one of the top qualities for a mentor.

Are you a good listener and communicator, or a motivational person who can inspire others? Are you resourceful, well organized, or able to offer constructive criticism? If you have one or more of these qualities, you are a good candidate to operate a retreat and to act as its mentor to guide your residents.

I remember meeting a mentor who lacked confidence in his mentoring talents. He had been journaling for 10 years, read most of the classics of literature, and had been writing short stories. I suggested he offer a journaling clinic to writers; three people registered; they then came back for his next workshop, titled "Develop Your Story." That was the beginning. At first, he was scared someone would want something he would not be able to provide. That is a common fear. On the contrary, nobody will ask you to edit their screenplay if you don't know anything about screenwriting!

Offer your experience and expertise, whatever that happens to be. If you happen to have a degree in literature or creative writing, this is even better as people will certainly benefit from it. Literary services are an important aspect in making a retreat a success. A simple way to begin offering them is to start by offering a workshop or a clinic on a topic you are very familiar. I strongly encourage mentors to offer at least two or three workshops their first year in order to create interest and build a clientele. I would go as far as offering a one- or two-day workshop a month, even if there are only two or three participants, and to develop a theme you are comfortable with. But remember, you are building your lifestyle with a business here. You are not on a marathon.

Remember this most basic and effective formula, which I always share with potential retreat operators in order for them to see a returning clientele:

1. Create a first face-to-face experience with writers via a workshop or a complimentary critique;
2. Create a bond: Identify and respond to their specific need right there on the spot;
3. Lead them back: Develop a workshop series; critique their work, conduct private coaching sessions during their next stay; edit their manuscript if they intend to publish or have their work produced; pitch their project to agent and publishers.

If you keep using this formula, rest assured that you will be busy for many years to come.

When you have finished your own evaluation you may decide to focus on and be responsible for the administrative side of the retreat business and not get involved in literary services. Have confidence in your decision, knowing that many writing coaches need your administrative skills. After reading this book, you may consider partnering with someone who wants to serve as mentor or coach for your retreat residents. When your administrative talents and gifts as a host are combined with the talents of a writing mentor your retreat will attract more writers, get more visibility, and generate more income. The information I provide throughout this book will assist you as the administrator of a retreat and will help you partner with a mentor for your greatest success. I also offer private, joint-venture consultation on matching partners in a retreat business.

Now that you know your vision, values, and strengths, you are ready to feed your potential residents by learning the ins and outs of putting on a writing retreat.

Chapter 5
Start-up Checklist

One of the first steps in starting your new business is to review your city/municipality, county, state/province and federal regulations on business and obtain any necessary licenses or permits. Below is a list of items and questions to consider in this early stage of your business. It is not all-inclusive. Requirements vary depending on the type, size, location, etc., of the business, so as you learn the regulations, you will come up with more items.

To learn and comply with the legal requirements affecting your type of business, ask about the following, first with your local (city/county/municipality), state/provincial or even federal governments:

- Licensing and permits; license fees and regulations are different for each city.
- Liability insurance
- Environmental and labor regulations
- Zoning regulations for the area in which you want to have your retreat business

Once you know the regulations and have met them, you will also want to determine the form of business organization most appropriate to your needs. A tax accountant can explain the different types of business entities (sole proprietorship, partnership, corporation, etc.) and the advantages and disadvantages of each. You also want to establish policies on salaries and hiring practices if you need to hire people.

Yes, it is important to get the start-up checklist and the professional advice you will need. However, try not to get trapped in these technicalities and always keep in mind that you cannot avoid taking risks in the business world. People with most rewarding lives are comfortable with insecurity. When I talk to self-employed professionals or small businesses going through a hard time, I often see that when things got tough, they ceased to do what they were doing when everything was working. They forget their vision and their passion. You must never forget that the biggest fortunes are built from risk. Your most beautiful moments are also achieved through risk. For example, you could not play it safe when you chose to have a child or to launch your career. You had to commit and go for it.

You must not let your need for security move you away from your pure vision. For example, the expression "marketing plan" can make you think, as part of the linguistic furniture, that you cannot do marketing without a plan. When you have a very well defined vision, you have to act upon events coming your way in order to reach your destination. Yes, you can always plan the path to follow and what you will need (business plan), but the more you are connected to your vision, the less you will need the "plans." When on vacation, do you waste time asking yourself how the chef prepared the meal at the restaurant? No! You order, eat, and enjoy.

Take a look at your life and remember the five best moments you wrote down earlier.

Those moments—were they not the ones where you said, "Whatever! I'll go for it!" or "I'm all in!" That marvelous reflex brought you the most beautiful experiences of your life—don't lose it. Go for it!

Chapter 6
Getting Started: The Venue

If you plan to purchase a property for your retreat, you need to decide if you are seeking a home to live in or simply a house with additional dwelling units, such as guest cottages, carriage houses, villas, mother-in-law apartments, etc. Do you want a year-round retreat or do you want a seasonal retreat? Educating and guiding homeowners and helping them to explore the various options is part of the services I offer.

You may skip this chapter if you already own or lease a property to run your business.

Analyze What You Need in a Property

Whatever your situation, the one thing you must have is good information to understand the implications of any important decisions. When it's time to buy a property for a retreat, many people struggle to find good information. And the last thing you want to do is rely entirely on people who are trying to sell you something. With a little bit of insight you can make informed decisions and avoid expensive mistakes. For instance, you need to decide the most profitable geographical areas and property types. Don't put your hard-earned cash on the line until you have finished reading this book. Even though I have several years of experience as a realtor in my region, I always encourage new homeowners to seek professional advice in their specific area if they are seeking to make an investment.

Choosing a Location

Determining the location is the primary step (assuming you have already decided how much money you plan to invest in a property). If you are unsure about the location, you might have to travel to several places or to any region or district that you have been considering as a place to establish your retreat for the next few years.

When we established the retreat in Colorado, we met the owner of five vacation homes that were only booked three months during the summer. They were located in the mountains but within a 10-minute drive to town and a half-hour drive to the airport. We decided this was perfect for our retreat. After a few weeks of negotiations we finally came to an agreement and signed a 10-year lease. Within two months, we began booking our 15 studios/rooms spread in the compound of five homes.

On the other hand, when we relocated the headquarters to Québec, Canada, I had several regions that would meet our lifestyle and needs. We traveled to all of them. I knew the Québec city region very well, since it was where I was born and lived until my twenties. It is 98 percent French. This would have been wonderful but would have been limited in terms of finding bookstores, libraries, and periodical resources in English. We eliminated this one, since we wanted to continue offering services in Shakespeare's language. There were two regions left to consider: the Laurentians and the Eastern Townships. The former had it all including easy access to the airport but our hearts were not vibrating when we stayed there. It was only when we took a full week to explore the Eastern Townships region that we felt at home. Its natural beauty reminded us of Colorado without the dramatic scenery of the gigantic mountains. The region offers lakes, rivers, rolling hills, and mountains. It is vibrant with artists and rich in creativity. We worked with a realtor and on our first tour we were scheduled to visit three properties. We knew at first sight that the third house was our future retreat—a centennial English cottage in the heart of a small community right on the border with the United States.

In your search, take time to explore the targeted area where you want to establish your retreat. Where ever the location you select, make sure that here you feel good and you know in your heart that it is the right place.

What Is the Property Market?

It is also a good idea to research the latest reports or news for a heads up on what is going on in the chosen property market and where property prices are heading. Do your own homework as information is power. Learn all about the issues that might affect you as a buyer, owner, and even eventually seller of a property in that area. Learn the actual costs of buying real estate. Search the Internet to find available properties of the type you want. Once you understand the market in your area and have some places in mind, it is time to get a real estate agent and get serious about finding your place.

Finding a Real Estate Agent

Eventually you will need a lawyer and other service providers, but first let's talk about the agent. No matter how educated you are about what's available on the market, a good real estate agent is essential—and can be hard to find. In my opinion, the best agent for you is an experienced professional who knows your market, will listen to you, and will conduct themselves in an ethical manner. You have many resources for finding a good agent: You can obtain realtors' directories; Google the top real-estate companies in the area; visit Open Houses where you can meet the agents in a relaxed environment and interact with them; and get referrals to good agents from your friends or colleagues.

Once you have chosen an agent, I strongly suggest you stay with the one you select—assuming you are happy with your choice—until you find a property.

Deciding What You Need

Sit with your agent and analyze what you need in the property intended to be a retreat business *and* your home. Your house is where you will live and where your guests will stay. Ask yourself and discuss with the agent how many bedrooms you will need—for you and for your customers. If you live in the same house as your guests, the flow, functions, and layout of the house is a major factor. You want to plan ahead in order to enjoy your life in your home, your business retreat, and your guests.

Let's say, for instance, that your prospective house has three bedrooms. Will one be for you and two for your guests, or two for you and one for the guests? Maybe you want to start with one for guests and expand later to two. Think about what will be the most comfortable way to start.

As you discuss what you need, be aware that you are creating your lifestyle. For that to be enjoyable, it is imperative you choose a place where you can create privacy for you and your family. Your quarters should be apart from the guest quarters or at least have some privacy so you are not sharing every minute of your life with your guests. I have been running retreats since 1998, and as much as I love it, I need my privacy even if only for a few minutes in the evening, in the morning to drink my coffee, or for a dinner with my friends. I have learned to make sure there is enough distance and walls between us that my life remains mine and is not shared with everyone under my roof. This need for privacy is a reality and is even more important if you share your life with a partner. I remember vividly one time when my ex-partner, acting as on-site mentor, needed some uninterrupted time to work on his own editing projects. He had to tiptoe to his office next to the residents' studios to get work done. We learned our lesson quickly and moved his office to the back of the house for more privacy.

The ideal situation is that the property you choose has a separate building for your guests. For example, when I co-founded the retreat in Colorado, we lived in the main lodge and writers stayed in the four houses spread within one mile of the lodge. Writers were welcome to use the great room of the main lodge at anytime to read and sip a coffee, discuss writing with other residents in front of the fireplace, and go back to their cottage later. The lodge was also where we conducted our workshops and group meetings, seminars, and private coaching sessions. This was ideal; we had total privacy and guests could spend long evenings sharing their work or simply sitting in front of a crackling fire in the great room.

The latest retreat I operated in Québec featured a different set up which is what most current retreats offer. Four rooms located on the second floor were reserved for guests and common areas on the first floor where we conducted workshops or other kinds of sessions. Our private quarters were located on the third floor as well as in the back of the house. When the hosts and the guests live in the same building you have to be very strategic in the allocation and use of the rooms in order for everyone to enjoy their privacy.

It will become clear in your discussions of what you need that several types of facility are appropriate for a retreat. It is your responsibility to decide what will be most suitable for you and your guests. For instance, a retreat may offer individual one-bedroom, one-bath, fully contained cottages or villas on a private compound, with the retreat operator living on-site or somewhere else. This is an excellent choice if you already own such a property or if you prefer not to live in the same building as your guests. However, depending on where you are located, the overhead costs (electricity, water, air conditioning, heating, property taxes, etc.) may be too costly. You need to investigate these prior to settling on that type of retreat. If you already own such property, you would greatly benefit by using it to cater to writers.

Keep in mind that writers, focused on their projects and working most of the day, cause much less wear and tear to properties than vacationers. Vacationing families and kids simply move around more, take more showers and baths, use the kitchen more, pots and pans, sheets, etc. Then again, if writers stay in their rooms or cottages or villas with the air conditioning or heat on all the time, this may increase your costs. It might cost more than having vacationers who are going to the beach, hiking, skiing or golfing all day. You may need to consider these aspects, depending on the climate where your property is located.

As you are looking for your retreat place in the area that appeals to you, do not be shy to talk to neighbors. If your agent is on a tight schedule, go back to the neighborhood on your own and ask questions about the community; go to the bakery or coffee shop; have a meal at the local restaurant; read the local newspapers; stop at the city hall to find out about permits, special programs for new homeowners, and special services available in the area, including the availability of Internet connection. You can also learn from people on Internet forums. You will be amazed at how much you can find out about positive and negative aspects of an area to help you in your decision.

Once you've made your choice and have bought a property, or, if you already owned the property, now, as a new or long-term retreat owner, it's time to get your place set up for your writers' retreat business.

Chapter 7
Retreat Cleaning, Renovating, Staging

Before decorating your retreat, first decide your budget for renovating and staging your house or retreat. Then ask what rooms are most important and how you can adapt your furniture to the residents' needs.

Do not hesitate to reorganize your home to change the function of a room if needed. I remember one retreat operator who had a difficult time identifying the proper room in her home for the writer. She mentioned she had an open loft that she and her husband used for relaxing for the past 10 years. It featured a 3-piece sofa, a TV, and a piano. It was kind of a den above the living room, next to their child's bedroom and bathroom. They had raised their child with this set up. Although it is sometime difficult to turn things upside down and now call it a writer's guest suite, this was the perfect solution to meet writers' needs and privacy. She was very proud to have created a new life for her loft!

First, Clean and Repair or Renovate; Second, Home Stage

Before staging the retreat facility, you need to de-clutter it, make any minor repairs that are needed, and clean it from top to bottom—windows, studio closets, kitchens, and bathrooms including inside cupboards & drawers. In the case of the woman mentioned above, first I suggested they remove the television and the large sofa and put a good writing table under the skylight, with a good reading lamp, two comfortable chairs, a couple of book shelves with reference books and magazines, and most importantly, to remove all the personal items, such as family pictures. Since they were now using this loft only once a month and the kid's bedroom was practically never used, their guest writer would have his/her own private bedroom to sleep even if it was small, a private bathroom and a private study room. Simple? Yes. Easy? Yes. She just created a comfortable place/retreat for a writer. You may say, I have two rooms I want to use for writers. That's great—you can offer as many as you decide to invite in your home. Just remember that peace and privacy of the retreat is the key and if you can create that with only one room when you begin, that is beautiful!

Bathroom fixtures, appliances, and floors should be hospital clean. Clear off and put away everything from the bathroom counter, desks, and closets. Make sure there are no personal items in bathroom cabinets. Remove all personal and religious items from common areas and working studios; replace them with reference books or writing magazines, classic paintings on the walls or none at all. Remember, writers are looking for space of their own to write!

At this stage, you have already acquired good reading lamps and comfortable chairs and allocated part of your budget on new linens, pillows, and bedspreads, unless you ask residents to bring their own. Caution: most writers expect to have everything they need in place when they search for a writing retreat. Do not be shy about shopping at garage sales, where you can find treasures for both the inside and the outside.

Now you are ready to prepare the space for your guests. Home staging means more than decorating and cleaning. It is about the art of creating moods. Staging can make your retreat look bigger, brighter, cleaner, warmer, more loving. And best of all, it makes writers want to stay and to come back in the future.

While I am not an accredited home-staging professional, with my years of experience in real estate and in running writing retreats I have time-tested suggestions about how to transform your house into a warm, inviting retreat that looks good, feels good, smells good, and conveys a creative and welcoming atmosphere. There's no limit to ways you can change a home and personalize it using a creative mind and developing a visual imagination. In other words, it's about adding the small details: the comma, the right adjective, the exclamation point, and, for simplicity, a stunning single quote of Hemingway!

I suggest you neutralize the decor by painting rooms a soothing, relaxing color; bring the outdoors inside with greenery and plants; create clean, crisp spaces; and arrange the furniture so there is plenty of room to walk around. Bathrooms should be spotless, airy, and delightful. One of my favorite habits is to put a basket filled with fancy soaps, lotions, and shampoos in the women's bathrooms. For the men, I offer baskets filled with practical and unusual gadgets or gourmet snacks.

The yard needs staging as well. For patios and writing decks, I bring in plants and potted flower and add additional color by setting mini-tables and comfortable chairs or benches under trees. I like to create themes. One summer I decorated in yellow and blue, which is the French country style of Provence. The following season I did a Southwest theme, with lots of cactus plants and Native American touches, so the guests would feel like they had just stepped into Arizona or New Mexico.

If you lack confidence in your ability to stage your retreat space, ask a friend or colleague to help you. If your budget allows, hire a professional stager, for which fees may range from $500 to $2,000 or more, depending on square footage and the number of rooms staged.

After you have completed preparing your facility, I cannot stress enough the importance of posting top-quality pictures on your Web page showing the working studios, writing desks and windows, and common areas. Your goal is Optimum First Impression.

Chapter 8
Marketing Strategy: An Overview

Marketing starts, ends, lives, and dies with your residents/customers. So in the development of your strategy, it is imperative that you forget about your dreams, about your visions, about your interests, about what you want—forget about everything but your customer—the writer and resident! When it comes to marketing, it is what the writer wants that matters. And what your customer wants is probably significantly different from what you *think* he wants. So find out what your customer actually wants and meet that need.

Good marketing is more than colorfully illustrated brochures or well-written newspaper advertisement. Rather, it is the process of developing a strategy to attractively present the services that you offer to interested and qualified customers. Knowing who are your existing or potential customers and what they want is essential to effective marketing.

Marketing to Your Territory

Of course, our website may bring writers from all over the world to your retreat, but first you may want to attract the writers living near your retreat. In the last ten years, the geographic location has become the key for writers to book a retreat. They occasionally choose a retreat for a writing vacation, but most of the times they just want to go away from home and drive to a retreat within reasonable distance—usually four or five hours maximum. This is a good reason not to neglect your city or region, your province or state market. I suggest you research the market for writers in your area. If your budget doesn't allow for a market analysis, you may consider hiring a graduate student to do it for you in an exchange of services.

You can also work with universities and colleges in your state or participate in local writers' conferences or writing seminars where you can give door prizes to stay at your retreat. I have done that on a regular basis in the past and it is a great way to promote your retreat. For example, we agreed with the conference organizers to display The Writers' Retreat name on each conference participant's badge holder (neck wallet type). We could not have asked better visibility to get our name out there directly to writers and authors. When they drew the door prize, lots of people already had heard about us and had seen our name or already stopped by our table display.

I contacted a few writers groups in the Denver area when I was operating our first retreat in Colorado. I suggested they invite us for a 10-minute talk at their luncheon. It was a great way to distribute our information flyers and to get to know the writers groups.

Steady promotion of yourself and your place, and especially persistence, is the key. Most retreat operators have a beautiful place for catering to writers and have creative talent to share with residents. Do not be shy to offer scholarship, grants, or anything that will bring people to you so they can advance their project or simply enjoy the quietness of the place to work solo. You may want to contact local magazines and newspapers to generate articles. Be creative. Instead of thinking, "Build it and they will come," think, "Promote it and they will come." And if they come, they should come back again and again! It takes patience and time to find creative ways to keep clients returning. Keep in mind that they need you and your place. Just go get them! Remain proactive and confident in your venture in any economic situation.

Designing and Promoting Your Program

Business cards / Letterhead / Logo

You need to create your business cards and letterhead. Even if you do not have a special event planned at this time, you want to have your business cards ready. For example, you never know whom you will meet while browsing at the bookstore. You need to carry them with you and give them to people you know: your hairdresser, your dentist, and your mechanic. Don't be shy about telling people that you just opened a new business—you will be amazed how many of them know someone with a writing project on the way. Business cards are made to give out, not to collect in your drawer!

You can create your business cards and letterhead yourself in a Word document or any other appropriate software. If you prefer a more professional look, ask a desktop publisher to create them for you. If you prefer not to have your home address on them, you can use a postal box or no address at all. However, you want to make sure to have at least your name, your business name, telephone number, e-mail, and the website address so people can reach you.

As for your letterhead, you may not need big boxes of letterheads, but you definitely need to be prepared should you need to write a letter. I have prepared a Word document in my computer so it is always ready to complete and print or to attach to an e-mail. See below an example of letterhead for your retreat.

Logo

You may already have created your logo, your lawyer has reviewed it to ensure that it does not infringe upon other trademark logo and has registered it. Most of retreats do not have a logo and that is perfectly fine! When you post your retreat on our network, you will be asked to post your "trademark" picture. This is the main picture of your retreat that appears on our website home page; this is how people will identify your retreat and will remember it. If you want to create your own logo, you can hire a desktop publisher or you can go to www.gotlogos.com for about $25 per logo or to www.99designs.com or to www.designoutpost.com or to www.killercovers.com and www.istockphoto.com.

You are prohibited from using The Writers' Retreat logo at anytime, as it is the propriety of The Writers' Retreat only. Please do not use it in your business.

Note: Most of the samples in this book are available to all retreat operators to download from our website; it may change from time to time.

Letterhead sample:

The Writers' Retreat
In Stanstead (Québec) Canada

15, Canusa Street
Stanstead (Québec)
J0B 3E5 Canada

Telephone: 819 876-0000—E-mail: info@writersre-treat.com—website: www.WritersRetreat.com

Promoting Your Literary Services

As part of your marketing strategy, you have to decide the literary services you will offer, establish its format (workshops, seminars, private coaching, placement services, etc.) and its schedule. Whatever your role is—speaker, facilitator (or you may invite guest speakers)—a good time to start offering your program is as soon as possible after you open your retreat.

You will want your program to generate interest in your retreat and to cover a mix of topics that, in addition to fitting your targeted clientele, to relate loosely to each other so that your audience can make connections and draw their own conclusions. For example, in our first years of operation, we offered the three workshops below on a regular basis. New writers registered and followed their mentor, progressing in a mutual understanding of the project, and most importantly, stayed loyal to us. The workshops were:

- **Story Realization:** To expand their story idea into a fully developed structure. Whether woven from whole cloth or based in reality, the story needs a shape, a clearly identifiable premise, and an empathetic main character. We invited them to come armed with their story idea or simply their reason for writing whatever it is they needed to write about.
- **Dynamics of the Dramatic Structure:** To demonstrate the interdependence of story ele-

ments. We planned this workshop before they started rewriting their first draft.

- **Self-Editing for Publication:** To learn to use successful techniques for editing their manuscripts in order to maximize its potential for publication. We escalated the tempo with thrilling demonstrations of success. It left them with a feeling that motivated them into action.

For example, you might want to start your program with two to four workshops or clinics in order to create a bond in their first meeting with their mentor. This is an important factor that provides consistency and a consistent value to the customer. It allows you to nourish the same clientele year after year in order to help them progress and reach their goal. If you offer the same workshop over and over again, your participants might lose interest, hence the idea of building a staircase effect by creating workshops 101, 102, 103, etc., so writers can step up and master their craft over time, progress and remain with their mentor as long as they wish until their project is polished and completed and ready for the publisher or agent.

Promotional Materials

When writing your promotional materials, pay attention to your wording. Anyone in a selling position should be very careful of making direct claims. Tom Hopkins, a master salesman says: "If you say it, it's a lie. If your prospect says it, it's the truth."

So instead of making the claim, "The *Self-Editing for Publication* workshop is the single-best way to get your novel polished and ready for publication," try this: "If you're serious about getting your book ready for publication, the *Self-Editing for Publication* workshop might be the answer."

The latter choice leaves your reader room to make a decision. It also encourages him to read on. If your prospect believes he's being pushed into buying or registering, he will discount your claims. Qualifying phrases not only smooth out your writing, they gently lead your reader to a decision.

Chapter 9
Proven, Successful Tools

Below are selected tools we offer to help you market to your targeted clientele:

The Writers' Retreat newsletter

The Writers' Retreat quarterly newsletter is an effective and easy way for retreat operators and mentors to connect with writers. Every quarter the newsletter gives you the opportunity to publish an article in which you can be opinionated and imaginative; this is your chance for potential residents to get to know you and to contact you directly. Writing an article that is of genuine interest and help to writers often results in new bookings. It creates a desire in readers to work with you on their project or simply to get to know you.

To further market your services, take advantage of social networking on sites such as Facebook, Twitter, LinkedIn. They are free opportunities to reach large numbers of people. You can build your network of writers and residents and communicate to them on a weekly basis about writing and your retreat! If you are interested in this avenue for marketing but are unfamiliar with it, there are lots of friendly and unintimidating guides and articles about social media on the Internet.

Posting your workshops online

When you join The Writers' Retreat network, you may post as many workshops as you want in the course of the year on our website. You may visit www.WritersRetreat.com to see all our retreat operators and mentors who post and publicize their workshops or clinics. Our website has a top Google ranking for writers' retreats. We constantly work on improving our visibility and positioning on the Internet.

Feedback forms

After your workshops, you may want your participants to fill out a feedback form to assess your performance and their satisfaction. Make careful note of their comments and needs so you can create exactly what they want in their learning process. I have seen mentors add yoga or breathing exercises during writing workshops after receiving feedback. Be open minded, flexible, and imaginative. You may also post on your website photos and videos of workshops (only with participants' written permission) for promotional purposes.

Brochure / Workshop flyer

It is a good idea to have a printed brochure for media inquiries or to distribute at events such as writers' conferences. Again, you can make your own if you do not need to print a large volume. Most businesses now use electronic brochures in pdf format, which can be sent easily by e-mail as an attachment or can be downloaded from your website.

You can easily create a one-page flyer pertaining to your retreat and your workshops and print it in color on a glossy paper.

Gift certificates

On occasion, you may receive requests from people who want to give attendance at your retreat as a gift to a partner, friend or colleague. So it's a good idea to have a personalized gift certificate already designed that you can send by mail or by e-mail. I have also used them as door prizes at events such as writers' conferences or seminars. I create them in PowerPoint, but you can also create them in specialized software or in Microsoft Word.

Website

Your website is an important piece of your marketing, which means you need to double check that it does a good job. Did you perfect your retreat description so it is inviting and inspiring, rather than sounding technical, like a spec sheet of a house for sale? Remember, you are creating your image, and you want people to be drawn to your writing, your bio, and your retreat. Be imaginative and inspiring; the simplest, well-described detail in a sentence may trigger a potential resident to become a long-term customer. Post your most beautiful pictures of the retreat. I've seen often just a picture of a bed. Of course, we want to see a bed, but maybe the corner of the bed would suffice, or the picture could include that beautiful, large window that opens onto the woodsy yard.

Examine your photographs, read your bio and your workshop descriptions. I want you to be honest with yourself on this—do you and your place stand out? What you leave out is as important as what you include in your descriptions.

Gift certificate sample:

Welcome to your Retreat!

As a participant at the

2010 Surrey International Writers' Conference

We are delighted to offer you

a complimentary week at

The Writer's Retreat in Stanstead, Québec, Canada

Validation required—See back of Certificate

www.WritersRetreat.com

The Writers' Retreat in Stanstead, Québec

15, Canusa, Stanstead (Québec) J0B 3E5—819 876-0000

www.WritersRetreat.com—info@writersretreat.com

[Back of Certificate]

- Certificate is valid for twelve (12) months starting December 15, 2010.
  Reservation subject to availability.

- Redeemable for one person for seven (7) nights lodging at The Writers' Retreat in Stanstead, Québec, Canada

- This certificate is non transferable, and will not be replaced if lost or stolen.

To validate this certificate please call or write at above address.

Chapter 10

Growing Your Business in a Productive, Assured Way

I often am asked by retreat operators, "How much money can I make?" or "Will I be earning $1,000 a month, $25,000 within 12 months?" Although it varies from person to person and depends on several factors, the answer boils down to how you bond with people, your personality and qualities, your services, and your marketing. Each retreat operator runs his or her business independently, and I do not ask about incomes. You need to be positive but realistic. Although money is important, if your sole aim in operating a retreat is to earn money, I am not sure it will survive. However, I can assure you that a retreat operator and mentor can make a good living with their retreat if they discover their true value and let others know about it.

For example, one year our former on-site mentor made $30,000 with only one resident writer who participated in one workshop and came back to stay at the retreat to work on a book. The writer then opted for three consecutive days of private mentoring during that week and came back five times the same year. The second year, the same writer opted to have the entire manuscript edited and then wanted help pitching her book at writers' conferences, writing query letters, contacting agents, and exploring forms of publication—all the placement services in general to get it published.

In order to develop a long-term clientele, let me share our success key with you: We continuously offered our residents a 15-page complimentary critique of a sample of their work. This has proved over the years to be the most effective way to acquire clients, grow our retreat business, and generate more income. Even if a resident does not enroll in a workshop, but only booked a stay at our retreat to write in peaceful surroundings, we offered to critique their work on-site or whenever they were ready. Because we knew that sometimes it is difficult for a beginner to share their writing, they could opt to send us their material for critiquing after their stay.

This basic service always has been a creative trigger for our residents: first, receiving their first critique of their work, and second, prompting them to take advantage of our services, whether our workshops or one-on-one sessions with a mentor, and eventually to return to the retreat and schedule a private-coaching session with the mentor. This is our way to assist and guide our residents and at the same time ensure they will continue working with their mentor on their project. With that one basic, free service, we created a returning, long-term client.

I strongly encourage you to provide that basic complimentary service for your residents, whether it is in fiction, poetry, journaling, nonfiction, screenwriting, playwriting, etc. And remember, the critique will be free, but all literary services coming out of it pay off many times over.

All your efforts are essential and ultimately rewarding when you see returning clients; your business will simply grow in a productive and assured way.

Chapter 11
Defining the Structure

As I mentioned earlier, our tools = structure = consistent value to residents. You want to use the tools effectively.

Establishing Your Fees

Retreat operators must know their value and worth and must understand supply and demand in order to establish their fees. Determining the going rates for services comparable to yours can be challenging and is the most difficult step for most retreat operators and mentors. One simple tactic is to call companies or consultants that offer similar literary services and find out their pricing for similar activities. Then compile a price list for your various services. Many self-employed writing mentors advertise their services on the web and a simple search on each of the services may bring up many web pages that list the price ranges. You do need to make sure they are quality, reliable organizations.

There are many acceptable methods to set your fees—a flat rate (or daily/weekly for lodging), an hourly rate, a project rate, or a combination of all three. Your fees can also be part of a package of several services, such as lodging, meals, coaching sessions, etc.

Overall, a pricing strategy should consider all of the costs—from maintenance to marketing—involved in producing the service. Your weekly studio rate, for example, should be based on these fixed and variable costs, plus some reasonable return on your investment. It is important to determine a competitive rate that covers expenses and allows the business to profit, if that is your goal. You can certainly look at the current retreats on The Writers' Retreat website and compare fees. Also, check with your local Small Business Administration for ideas. They have numerous volunteers on staff with experience in the business world that are more than willing to discuss pricing strategies with those just getting started in the business. Finally, specific features and services at your retreat may require minor adjustments upward (private deck, complimentary food or meals, etc.) or downward (shared bath, no Wi-Fi, etc,) in price.

Once you decide your fees, establish your payment, cancellation and refund policies. Display them clearly in your material, on your Web page, and in your confirmation of reservation, registration, or contract agreement.

To evaluate your facility and surrounding market accurately and, more importantly, reach a balance between your service and your rates, you simply need to give great value and quality while honoring your own value and services.

Daily Operations and Systems

Your retreat business will stand out and will find and keep customers, profitably when you establish an effective system of management and practice it year after year. In order to help you start your business, the Writers' Retreat provides a model and basic tools. Once you join the Writers' Retreat network, you will have our tools along with access to an online administrative account, where you will find templates and materials you can download so you can start your business immediately without spending the time and money to create them yourself.

Greetings / Retreat Name / Signature

One of the first tools we offer relates to your very first contact with a potential customer—your telephone greeting. I suggest you first remove your personal greeting on your voice mail and record a short, professional greeting for your retreat. You may want to have it in two languages, depending on where you are located.

The greeting needs to include the name of your retreat. It is a good idea to keep the name simple, since it will probably eventually affect your domain name should you develop your own website. You can adjust it to fit your place and reflect your personality. Smile while you are recording the message—it makes a big difference.

A sample:

Hello,
You have reached Alex and The Writers' Retreat in [...], please leave a brief message and your telephone number and we'll get back to you shortly. Thank you and have a wonderful creative day!

Since you may receive inquiries the same day you join The Writers' Retreat network, and you need to respond immediately, the second task is to create your e-mail signature. Anyone in business needs to have their full name and telephone number and e-mail address in every e-mail they send. Do not assume that the person to whom you are writing already has it. Make it part of all your replies, even to those you know. Believe me, it is much more professional to include full information in your e-mails, and people appreciate it. Let's just do simple things that people appreciate.

Below is an example of an e-mail signature you can create:

Micheline Côté
The Writers' Retreat in Stanstead, Québec
819 876-0000
www.WritersRetreat.com
info@writersretreat.com

Confirmation of Reservation by E-mail

Now that you have pitched your place and your retreat, you have your first booking or workshop registration, either over the phone or by email. (In that process, you asked them about their writing interests, including their genre.) Immediately after you have received the deposit by credit card, PayPal, or check, it is very important to confirm the reservation in writing via e-mail. It does not matter if you took it by telephone or e-mail, you need to confirm in writing.

When sending out an e-mail Confirmation of Reservation, make sure you use the HTML format so any links will work. I suggest you follow up with a telephone call or request a *Reply* to your message to make sure your e-mail message is not sitting in their junk mail.

Here is a sample of confirmation of reservation or registration:

> E-mail confirmation of reservation—-—S A M P L E
>
> Dear [ ],
>
> Thank you for your reservation. We are delighted you chose The Writers' Retreat in [ ] to work on your project. Welcome to your retreat!
>
> PLEASE PRINT THIS MESSAGE, THIS IS YOUR CONFIRMATION
>
> Name & address:
> Joe Smith
> 3363 Edinburgh
> Boston, MA 00000
> Telephone: 300-781-2000
> joesmith@gmail.com

Arrival date: Sunday, June 1st, 2011
Check in time: 2:00 p.m.
Departure date: Sunday, June 15, 2011
Check out time: 12:00

Weekly residency—7 nights:
Consultation: $595.00
Tax: (included)
Total: $595.00
Deposit: $200 (Check # 202)
Balance due upon arrival: $495.00

If there is any discrepancy in the above information, please notify us immediately.

Material: Bring all the material you will need for your retreat including CD Rom. To make sure you have a productive stay, please bring all your necessary equipment and accessories.

Wireless Internet: Accessible throughout the retreat and in your studio; so, bring your laptop!

Printer: We provide 25 complimentary pages—please bring your paper (for laser printer) if you need to print more than 25 pages; printing cost is $0.04 per page. Feel free to bring your small portable printer.

Meals: Coffee & juice included in the morning and one complimentary dinner; residents have access to the kitchen to cook light meals. There's a mini fridge for residents to store refreshments & snacks; assorted teas available. There are a few restaurants in Stanstead—one within walking distance; many more in Newport, VT—a 10-minute drive and about 30 restaurants in charming Magog—25 minutes via the scenic road. There's also a grocery store 2 miles away as well as a traditional French bakery cooking the old-fashioned way.

Visitors: No overnight visitors are allowed. Smoking outside only.

Nota: Our residents receive a complimentary critique of a sample of their work (15 pages) from on-site mentor.

Retreat address:
15, Canusa Street, Stanstead (Québec) Canada J0B 3E5

CLOSEST MAJOR AIRPORTS:
Pierre-Elliott Trudeau Int'l Airport in Montréal (Québec); (1 ½ hour drive to the Retreat on Highways 10 and 55 South): http://www.admtl.com/

Major car rental companies are located at both above airports.

If you drive:
Directions: Coming from NY, CT, MA, ME, NH—In Vermont, take I-91 North towards the Canadian border. Pass the first Newport Exit and take exit # 28 (Highway 105 East) to Derby Center. Drive through Derby Center; turn left (North) at the intersection (dead end) of Highway 5 and continue through the village of Derby Line. After clearing Canadian customs, turn left at the first stop sign (Railroad St.) towards Beebe (247 North), drive 2 miles. From Burlington, it's about 90 minutes; from Boston, four hours.

TOURISM INFORMATION
Eastern Townships Region: http://www.easterntownships.cc/anglais/accueil.html
Province of Québec: http://www.bonjourquebec.com/anglais/index.html

Payment terms: COPY & PASTE WHAT IS POSTED ON YOUR WEB PAGE. It has to be the same to protect you and your guest.

Cancellation policy: COPY & PASTE WHAT IS POSTED ON YOUR WEB PAGE. It has to be the same to protect you and your guest.

If you have any questions, please contact us.

We look forward to meeting you!

Micheline Côté
The Writers' Retreat in Stanstead, Québec
819 876-0000
www.WritersRetreat.com
info@writersretreat.com

Bibliography

Now that you secured your first reservation, I encourage you use a portion of your budget to start building a library of reference books for your clientele. During the registration process you found out about the writer's project and what authors they like. You can now decide what books to display in your library the first time. Buy new or used books that are relevant. You can even borrow books of interest to your first resident.

Remember, the value you offer comes in the small details. Choosing the right book for your guest adds value to your customer service. With each new resident you will look for a new range of books and gradually build your library as you accept reservations. This is a practical way to select appropriate books for your guests.

Besides building a library, you also can plan ahead and start a special shelf dedicated to the books of your future-published residents. You will be surprised how many will get published over the years of operation of your retreat. They deserve recognition, so ask them to send you a signed copy. Moreover, why not develop a dedicated page for them on your website that you could title "Friends of the Retreat." This gives them additional visibility they will appreciate and highlights the long-term value of your services.

*Greeting your guest*s

You want to make sure to greet your guests in person on arrival—'"*Welcome to The Writers' Retreat {your retreat name}!*" Do not be hesitant to go outside to meet them when they arrive, sometimes the right entrance is not obvious to them when the retreat is a private home. Find out if they had a good trip and ask if the directions given were clear so you can improve them if needed. Always offer to help guests bring in their luggage and other items they have to carry in. Prior to showing guests to their room or studio, give a quick tour of the common areas, such as living room, library, kitchen, garden, etc., so they see the facility right away and feel more at ease. They will not feel like an intruder on your privacy once they know where to settle and where the fridge or pantry are located if they want to bring in food, for example. And take time to show them details, such as how to access a hidden switch, the music, the porch lights, etc., so they do not have to ask you everything. Introduce your pets, especially dogs so they do not bark at your guests when they pull in the driveway.

Once they have seen their working studio, it will not take them long to settle in. They may want to grab a bite at a nearby restaurant or to buy food at the grocery if your retreat does not offer meals. Keep in mind that they have been traveling, are probably tired, and want to settle in and be left alone after you've shown them the facility.

If you are using your home as a retreat, you may be worried about having strangers in your own house. Start developing your instincts. I have welcomed writers in my house for many years now, and I know the moment someone puts a foot in my door if I can trust that person. It is easy to develop your instinct; just listen to your feelings and you will know what to say or to do. If you have doubts about someone, it does not mean the person is bad, but it may mean you have to be diligent for a couple days until that person gains stability with the atmosphere of your retreat. Remember, they are also coming to a new environment and do not know the house or who is living in it. Keep in mind it is *your* house, and if you are really uncomfortable with someone's attitude, you can always thank them, refund their money, and ask them to leave. In all these years, I have only had one person I did not trust completely. The key is to open your heart, remain positive about what you do, and stay alert to what's going on around you and in your house.

House rules

I recommend you print out your house rules as guidance during their stay. However, do not over do it; I have seen retreats where there is a note on every corner. I strongly suggest you avoid this, as it is annoying and make your guests feel they are intruding in your space. Instead, write your rules on one piece of paper and display it in each private studio only.

Next is an example that you can create on your letterhead:

> Welcome to your Retreat!
> **Retreat Rules**...Please take a minute to read!
> You may use the kitchen for light meals; we appreciate you cleaning up when you are done. Feel free to use the mini-fridge in the dining room to store refreshments & snacks; plates/silverware, provided in the cabinet, where you may also store non-perishables (there is some additional space in the kitchen). We appreciate your eating in the dining room—no meals or cooking in your studio except for beverages & snacks. If you need to buy food, there is a grocery store (IGA) on Fairfax (next to Highway 55, across from Subway & Imperial Restaurant). Check our In-house Information binder for local restaurants.

If you have questions and we are not present at the front office, please leave a note on the desk. If you need to print anything, please e-mail your material or leave your CD at the front desk, and we will print it for you.

Wireless Internet: To access the Internet from your laptop, the code is 2926.

For the sake of everyone in the house, please use cellular phones in your studio only or outside. If you need to briefly use the Retreat private telephone, please ask first—this is our private line. You will need a calling card for long distance calls.

Room cleaning: Since you will be in your studio most of the day, we will work around your writing time to refresh your room (2-3 times a week). We appreciate your thinking about the next person using the bathroom when you're finished. As a courtesy to everyone, please keep a low voice in the house, be gentle when closing doors (this is a centennial house), remove hard-sole shoes. We appreciate your respecting everyone's privacy.

There's no "better" time to write at the Retreat: Our residents work day & evening, sometimes straight through the night. So feel free to make the most of your stay. Now, you're on your own...let's write!

Enjoy your stay!

In-House information binder / Retreat guest book

I suggest you put together an in-house information binder pertaining to local restaurant menus, coffee shops, book stores, libraries, if applicable. It is a good idea to renew these restaurant menus on a regular basis as they may change. You can also include press clippings if you wish. It is important to keep the book updated. You may want to organize a local tourist-information binder or display table for them to consult if they wish to explore the region during their stay.

Below is a sample cover for your in-house information binder:

Welcome to your Retreat!

Dear Writer and Resident,

At The Writers' Retreat in [ ], we take great pride in ensuring that you are completely comfortable and satisfied with the accommodations and services we offer. Your business is extremely important to us and we are committed to exceeding your expectations.

While you are staying with us, we invite you to browse the Author's Gallery, which offers an array of reference books to stimulate and assist you in your project.

It is our privilege and our pleasure to be looking after you while you are staying with us, but we also want to leave you lots of privacy. If you need anything at all, please let us know.

Again, welcome to The Writers' Retreat in [ ] where literary service and creative environment go hand in hand.

Happy writing!

The Writers' Retreat in Stanstead, Québec—www.WritersRetreat.com

Guest book

You also want to create a retreat guest book for guests to sign. This is where they show their appreciation, testimonials, comments, reviews that will be useful for you to improve your services or to use for promotional purposes. However, you want to make sure that your guests know that you may use their quotes in your promotional material, so indicate it clearly at the beginning of your guest book.

Chapter 12
The Working Environment

As I have said, it is very important to provide comfortable and clean lodging to your residents, including a comfortable desk and chair as well as good reading lamps. You may even want to keep battery-operated lamp in case of a power outage. A working retreat is very different than a bed and breakfast. For example, writers prefer not to be interrupted so you can clean their rooms. You will have to work around *their* schedule to refresh their room, empty their waste basket, remove dirty cups and glasses, and change towels. Take the opportunity to do it while they are having breakfast or have gone for a walk. Try not to miss doing this, even if they say they do not need it, because it is your home too and because other residents do not appreciate rooms that smell stale. I suggest you offer full maid service at least weekly and on a daily basis if your retreat is located in a warm climate. Cleaning up, even if it is just to change towels, also gives you a reason to go in their studio/room to keep an eye on what is going on.

I remember one resident who made more than a mess in his studio in only three days of my not being able to refresh it. He checked in just before Christmas, and I went away for three days; Tony took over in my absence, and the resident told him not to bother, that he was fine without cleaning his room during the holidays. So when I came back at 10:30 p.m., the guest was out visiting friends. I decided to refresh the room before he got back.

"Why don't you wait tomorrow?" Tony asked.

"I saw before I left that he messes up easily, so I'd better have a peak," I answered.

The smell of rotten food hit me right when I opened the door. I found a chicken carcass on the corner of the desk, lettuce and crackers on the floor, and one leg of the bed broken. I yelled so loudly I alarmed the whole house! I considered asking him to leave the house, but instead, I made it clear that I did not want any food in the studio before his departure two days later. That was an isolated case in all these years welcoming writers in my home.

Your On-Site Technology

No matter where they are staying, writers are starting to demand the very latest in technology. Residential retreats can be ahead of the game by integrating technology into their design and anticipating the technology that will make their guests' lives easier during their stay. Last summer, I went camping on the coast of Maine and no matter where we were on the five-acre campground, the guests had access to the Internet. As consumer technology becomes more affordable, guests are no longer impressed by flat-screen desktop computers, integrated CD players, etc.; they have that at home. What does impress them is when the technology improves the service, which in turn improves their experience.

Most writers bring their laptop computers to retreats, so you do not need to have a computer on-site for them or a CD/DVD player. Accessing the Internet is usually the first thing they want to do when they settle in their studio, so have the written instructions on how to connect on their desk. You will have sent them all the material they needed to bring (portable printer, paper, Ethernet cable, etc.) in their confirmation of reservation. Most writers will bring their portable printer, but it is helpful to have one available on-site if possible. You also want to make sure you have a "tech guy" they can call if needed.

Customer Service—A Typical Day

One of the things retreat operators learn is the importance of customer service. A pioneer in our retreat network, who is an expert on customer services, advises:

The time between when a guest first inquires about a stay and when they book a date, and ultimately when they first arrive is critical in terms of actually moving forward with getting to know the guest and setting up what kind of experience they will have at the retreat. I strive for an inviting tone, in that I express interest in who they are and what they are working on. I also share how I feel my retreat might be a suitable place for them to write. The personal touch has proved to make a difference in the process.

Also, having the potential guest complete an in-depth application with questions that range from contact information, emergency numbers, a brief word about themselves, their goals on their stay, what they are writing on, if/how they handle writer's blocks, dietary/other needs, health issues, etc. has been very useful in terms of getting a sense of the guest and tailoring a stay that will fit for each client individually.

I also find it valuable to have pow wow's with each guest at arrival and at departure. I first give a tour of the premises and share how things operate (i.e., sound system, dishwasher, office machines, washer/dryer, etc.) We also set a specific time to sit down after they settle in to discuss their writing goals for their stay. That way, they are clear on their writing direction, and they give voice to what they want to accomplish.

The time spent together after critiquing their 15 pages of writing has also proved useful for guests, because in addition to reading my notes on their writing sample, we are able to discuss the writing sample together. When they are about to depart, I ask each guest to sign my guest book (I use this book for testimonials for marketing), we discuss how their stay went, and we do a walk-through before their deposits are returned.

This personal touch along the way from beginning to end can make for an enjoyable and comfortable stay for each guest!

Create your uniqueness

You want to create your uniqueness in customer service, because it is a vital factor of this business. For example, responding promptly to inquiries is a key to getting bookings; it affects your customer service and of course your credibility. If you do not respond immediately, writers will go somewhere else. When you receive a request by email that includes the writer's telephone number, grab the phone and call them. You will be surprised how much they appreciate getting an immediate response "from a live person"—you. Always follow up the call with an e-mail. Remember, this is your first contact with the writer, so take advantage of it. Take the time to respond with details, using full sentences; do not insert your responses within the sender's text. You are talking to writers here, so please, have a sense of decorum and be meticulous. You have a chance to pitch your retreat here, just like you would pitch your project to an agent or to a publisher, so do it! Ask them questions about their writing, so they have a reason to respond and you can establish a connection; ask if you can have their telephone number, and call them; writers appreciate our taking time to talk to them. Pitch your place and your services with passion—be descriptive in your e-mail, sell yourself and your place as a place they dream to go to write and learn, to invest in their writing. Give them incentives to choose your place: one additional hour of consultation, an additional free night when they book seven nights, a free complimentary critique, one dinner on the house, bikes, massage available on-site, fresh daily fruits. Then ask THE final question: "How would you like to secure your space now, while we have availability?" And don't forget to thank them immediately for considering your retreat, even if they did not book right away!

Your customer service affects your guests' experience and impacts how many will return and/or refer their friends or colleagues.

Follow Up with Residents

It's important to follow up with past residents, and to call potential ones, rather than assume people will just call or connect again if they want to reserve. As in any business, following up at least monthly with all your customers will be stimulating, and they will see you care about their project. Follow up in a timely manner; when you have spare time, call them to say hello and see how they are doing with their writing. This helps you build and solidify your clientele. Talk to them on a regular basis. They will be appreciative—writers like to be pampered like anybody else. This is a way to do it, as long as you are sincere and really want to help them and your business. Follow up may bring a repeat resident for several consecutive years!

Chapter 13
Can You Stand Out in the Crowd?

Standing out from the crowd can give your retreat a competitive edge to succeed and, of course, make money. When you either have a unique service or a unique way of delivering that service, you give people a reason to talk about it. To achieve that, you have to come up with some angle, something no one else is doing. A good publicity stunt, for example, can have an avalanche effect on your retreat earnings and website's traffic. So can empathy to a guest in need of your refined attention.

When I lived in Los Angeles, I had to present a writing assignment to my creative-writing professor at UCLA; I was exhausted from too many hours of work and just wanted a quiet place to complete my writing assignment. I drove five hours to a retreat overlooking the valley. By the time I walked into the house, the sun was setting, and the garden was dark. Instantly, something told me that I was in a special place. I practically melted with delight.

Jennifer, the owner, appeared at the door dressed in a soft green sweater and a pair of jeans; a matching green ribbon held her hair back from her glowing face. "Welcome to the Retreat," she said, smiling warmly. She invited me in and showed me around—the sofa at the far side of the room against the wall, the massive fieldstone fireplace with a roaring fire. She showed me to my room—it was perfect!—and pointed out the binder with all the restaurants in the area. Then we went back to the main entrance, where she showed me my parking space and offered to assist with my luggage, laptop, a box of pads and books. I couldn't believe the ease with which it all happened. I dropped my stuff in my room and walked 10 minutes to the closest restaurant. The meal was as delightful as everything I had experienced so far, and the owners of the restaurant were expecting me. Evidently, Jennifer had called to reserve a table for me. I returned to the retreat, noting on the way that a soft light had been turned on in my room.

By the time I got there, the night had become chilly. I was looking forward to a nice bath before going to bed and reading. Somebody had guessed my wishes! A large candle was lit in the bathroom, the quilt was turned down on the bed, and the pillows were plumped, with a mint resting on one. On the night table stood a bookmark. I picked it up and read: *Welcome to your retreat. I hope will be enjoyable. If there is anything I can do for you, please don't hesitate to let me know. Jennifer.*

As I drifted to sleep that evening, I felt very well taken care of. It was not the candle, the mint, or the reservation at the restaurant that did it. It was that somebody had heard me.

Very often, I read this comment from residents in my guest book: "You provided just the setting I needed to think of myself as a writer and get into the mode;" or "I felt like a real writer here." This is simple, they want to feel they are writers and that they are staying at a writers' retreat! So, don't hesitate to pamper them. Isn't it what you would like?

You will create an atmosphere in which the retreat is not just a retreat but also an expression of who you are, a symbol of what you believe in and the respect you have for writers. On a day-to-day basis, your retreat will express those beliefs and attitudes.

Conclusion

That's it folks. I hope these guidelines give you a good flavor of what retreat operating is all about and what each stage of your project entails. I have tried my best to give you accurate information that you can use when you embark on this project.

But does it work? Will the retreat business work for you?

My answer is a resounding "Yes!" It does work as long as it gets your full engagement. It can't be done half-heartedly. And it can only be done compassionately. You must remember your aim and your standards in order to continue it. The retreat can become a symbol for the life you wish to live, a visible manifestation of who you are and what you believe.

An old Chinese proverb says:
When you hear something, you will forget it.
When you see something, you will remember it.
But not until you do something, will you understand it.

It's time to act. And when you do, there will be nothing left to think about. Until then, it's just another good idea, just another creative thought.

It's time to turn your good idea into your reality!

TESTIMONIALS

"My Writer's Well retreat in Georgia is now beginning to gain more momentum. It is a process learning the ropes and I am still learning.

I think the key is to maximize marketing strategies to drive writers to your retreat—be it the website, a newsletter, workshops, giveaways, whatever it takes that you are comfortable with to brand your name and make sure writers know you exist.

I am now going into my fourth year and have thankfully had writers now from as far away as Ghana, but it is still a process growing the retreat.

The good news is I am still in business!"

– Adilah Barnes, Sharpsburg, Georgia, USA

"I have been with The Writers' Retreat for a few years and can say that they most definitely have an insider's perspective on why writers go to retreats and what writers are expecting. The Writers Retreat understands the sensitive nature of the relationship between writers and their writing coaches and helps retreat owners structure their business to meet writers' needs.

The end result is a working relationship between writing and on-site editor that is rewarding in a myriad of ways."
– Mary Ann Henry, Folly Beach, South Carolina, USA

"A friend told me about The Writers' Retreat. That's when I met Micheline Côté, and began to learn about how to succeed as a retreat operator.

Ms. Côté's experience as a retreat operator, realtor, saleswoman, and writer was invaluable for me. Her suggestions over the years have helped me to think like a business woman; throughout our relationship, she's provided practical ideas and suggestions that leveraged a big return.

Ms. Côté has encouraged me to add personal touches to my retreat. With her help, I understand that the perfection of the retreat and the desire to serve the newly arrived writer have led me to enjoy a steady flow of happy, productive writers to my retreat in Vermont."
– Julia Shipley, Craftsbury, Vermont, USA

Made in the USA
Middletown, DE
10 May 2015